THIS CANDLEWICK BOOK BELONGS TO:

calf

recorder

ball

tree

jump rope

pig

xylophone

basket

duck

carrots

undershirt

kite

flip-flops

bubbles

toast

sheep

drum

paints

brushes

Teddy

sunglasses

blocks

party hats

clock

bucket

bananas

book

crayons

balloons

birds

picture

shovel

socks

slippers

cake

towel

duck

sand castles

doll

sweater

triangle

flowers

lemonade

chick

boiled egg

sponge

panties

apples

For Carlos

First U.S. paperback edition 1994
First published in Great Britain in 1991 by Walker Books Ltd., London.

ISBN 1-56402-042-8 (hardcover)
ISBN 1-56402-285-4 (paperback)
Library of Congress Cataloging-in-Publication Data is available.
Library of Congress Catalog Card Number 91-71817

10 9 8 7 6 5 4 3 2 1

Printed in Hong Kong

The pictures for this book were done in watercolor and ink.

Candlewick Press
2067 Massachusetts Avenue
Cambridge, Massachusetts 02140

WORDS AND PICTURES

Reading with Picture Clues

SIOBHAN DODDS

CANDLEWICK PRESS
CAMBRIDGE, MASSACHUSETTS

Getting Dressed

First I put on my undershirt

and panties,

then my  sweater

and  overalls,

and last my socks

and  shoes.

Breakfast

I have a  bowl of cereal

and a boiled egg.

Daddy always has a cup of coffee.

Mommy likes  toast

and  jam.

School

We have  crayons

and  paints

and brushes and 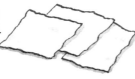 paper, and

we make   pictures

to put on the wall.

Playtime

Jason plays with his  ball,

Mary has her  jump rope,

Claire and Lucy put

the  doll to bed,

and I make a house

with  blocks.

In the Park

There are lots of  flowers

and birds,

and I like feeding the  ducks.

Once my  kite

got stuck in a  tree.

At the Beach

I like wearing my  sunglasses

and my  flip-flops.

I make  sand castles

with my bucket

and  shovel.

Shopping

Mommy puts the potatoes,

 carrots, and bananas

in her  basket.

I carry the peas,

 mushrooms, and  apples

in mine.

On the Farm

I feed the  hens and

chicks

and help to take care of

the  pig, the  sheep,

and the  calf.

At a Party

We drink  lemonade

and eat cookies and cake.

We all wear  party hats

and have balloons

to take home.

Music Time

Our teacher plays the piano,

Mary is learning the  recorder,

I play the triangle,

Jason plays the  xylophone,

and Lucy bangs the drum.

Bath Time

I blow 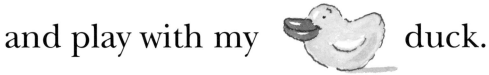 bubbles

and play with my duck.

Mommy washes me with soap

and a sponge

and dries me with a  towel.

Bedtime

I take off my  slippers

and get into  bed

with  Teddy.

Mommy reads me a book.

The  clock says 7 o'clock.

Good night!

calf

tree

recorder

jump rope

ball

pig

xylophone

basket

duck

carrots

undershirt

kite

flip-flops

bubbles

toast

sheep

drum

paints

brushes

Teddy

sunglasses

blocks

party hats

clock

bucket

balloons

bananas

book

crayons

birds

picture

shovel

slippers

socks

cake

towel

duck

sand castles

doll

sweater

triangle

flowers

lemonade

chick

boiled egg

sponge

panties

apples

SIOBHAN DODDS has illustrated a number of picture books for children, but she has always had a passion for rebus books. "They are the books that stand out in my mind from my childhood," she says, "and I've wanted to do one myself for a long time — which is how this picture dictionary came about." She is also the author of *Grandpa Bud*.